Science Builders

All about Matter

by Mari Schuh
Consulting Editor: Gail Saunders-Smith, PhD

Consultant: Joanne K. Olson, PhD
Associate Professor, Science Education
Center for Excellence in Science & Mathematics Education
Iowa State University, Ames

CAPSTONE PRESS
a capstone imprint

Pebble Plus is published by Capstone Press,
1710 Roe Crest Drive, North Mankato, Minnesota 56003.
www.capstonepub.com

Library of Congress Cataloging-in-Publication Data
Schuh, Mari C., 1975–
  All about matter / by Mari Schuh.
    p. cm.—(Pebble plus. Science builders)
  Summary: "Simple text and full-color photographs provide a brief introduction to matter and its properties"—Provided
by publisher.
  Includes bibliographical references and index.
  ISBN 978-1-4296-6068-6 (library binding)
  ISBN 978-1-4296-7105-7 (paperback)
  ISBN 978-1-4914-9929-0 (saddle stitch)
  1. Matter—Properties—Juvenile literature. 2. Matter—Juvenile literature. I. Title. II. Series.
  QC173.36.S38 2012
  530—dc22   2010053930

Editorial Credits
Erika L. Shores, editor; Bobbie Nuytten, designer; Wanda Winch, media researcher; Laura Manthe,
    production specialist

Photo Credits
Capstone Studio: Karon Dubke, 11, 19; Shutterstock: Albert Lozano, 1, 22-23, 24, ARENA Creative, 17, Danylchenko
Iaroslav, cover, 7, Lori Sparkia, 15, Pigprox, 13, Songquan Deng, 9, studiots, 5; Thinkstock, 21

Note to Parents and Teachers

The Science Builders series supports national science standards related to physical science.
This book describes and illustrates matter. The images support early readers in understanding
the text. The repetition of words and phrases helps early readers learn new words. This book
also introduces early readers to subject-specific vocabulary words, which are defined in the
Glossary section. Early readers may need assistance to read some words and to use the Table of
Contents, Glossary, Read More, Internet Sites, and Index sections of the book.

Table of Contents

What Is Matter?

Your bed, books, and house are matter. Everything in the whole world is matter.

Forms of Matter

Matter is anything that
takes up space.
Matter can be a solid,
a liquid, or a gas.

Solids keep their shape.

Rocks, trees, and ice cubes

are solids.

Liquids often feel wet and do not have their own shape. A liquid takes the shape of what holds it. Milk, water, and shampoo are liquids.

Gases have no shape.
Gases spread to fill the space
they are in. Air is made
of gases. You can feel air
move on windy days.

Changing Matter

Matter can change forms.

Solids can turn into liquids.

Ice cream melts on a hot day.

Liquids can turn into solids.

Liquid water turns into

ice cubes in a freezer.

Liquids can turn into gases.

Boiling water changes

from a liquid into a gas.

You can see, touch, taste,

and smell matter.

Matter is all around you.

Glossary

boil—heated until bubbling; water boils when it reaches 212 degrees Fahrenheit (100 degrees Celsius)

gas—a form of matter that spreads to fill any space that holds it

liquid—a form of matter that takes the shape of its container; liquids can be poured

matter—anything that takes up space and has mass

solid—a form of matter that has its own shape

Read More

Lindeen, Carol. *Solids, Liquids, and Gases.* Nature Basics. Mankato, Minn.: Capstone Press, 2008.

Royston, Angela. *Solids, Liquids, and Gases.* My World of Science. Chicago: Heinemann Library, 2008.

Weir, Jane. *Matter.* Mission, Science. Mankato, Minn.: Compass Point Books, 2009.

Internet Sites

FactHound offers a safe, fun way to find Internet sites related to this book. All of the sites on FactHound have been researched by our staff.

Here's all you do:

Visit *www.facthound.com*

Type in this code: 9781429660686

Super-cool stuff!

Check out projects, games and lots more at
www.capstonekids.com

Index

Word Count: 151
Grade: 1
Early-Intervention Level: 18